THE MOON

OUR NEAREST NEIGHBOR

Bruce Betts, PhD

Lerner Publications ◆ Minneapolis

THE PLANETS AND MOONS IN OUR SOLAR SYSTEM ARE OUT OF THIS WORLD. Some are hotter than an oven, and some are much colder than a freezer. Some are small and rocky, while others are huge and mostly made of gas. As you explore these worlds, you'll discover giant canyons, active volcanoes, strange kinds of ice, storms bigger than Earth, and much more.

The Planetary Society® empowers people around the world to advance space science and exploration. On behalf of The Planetary Society®, including our tens of thousands of members, here's wishing you the joy of discovery.

Onward,

Bill Nye

Bill Nye
CEO, The Planetary Society®

Table of Contents

CHAPTER 1

OUR NEIGHBOR IN SPACE

We live on Earth. The Moon is our neighbor in space. A moon is a body that orbits a planet or other body in space. Moons are also called natural satellites.

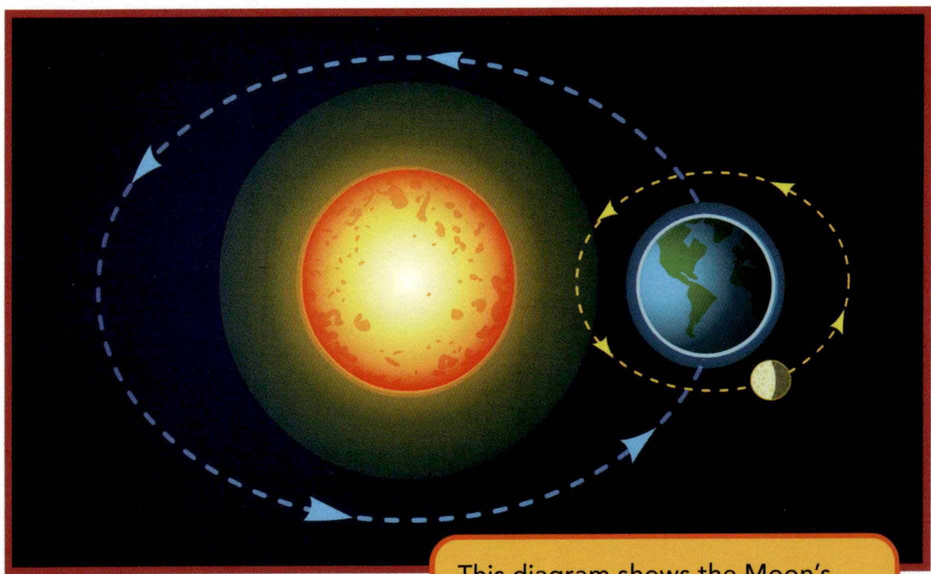

This diagram shows the Moon's orbit around Earth and Earth's and the Moon's orbit around the Sun.

The Moon goes everywhere Earth goes. The Moon orbits Earth. Together, the Moon and Earth orbit the Sun.

THE MOON FAST FACTS

Size	Could fit about fifty Moons inside Earth
Distance from Earth	About 250,000 miles (400,000 km)
Length of day	About thirty Earth days or one Earth month
Length of year	365.25 Earth days

Meet Earth's Moon

The Moon is much smaller than Earth. About fifty Moons would fit inside Earth. If Earth were the size of a basketball, the Moon would be about the size of a tennis ball.

The size of Earth (*left*) compared to the Moon (*right*)

Moon vs. USA
The Moon is about as wide as the United States or Europe. See how the United States lines up with the Moon in this image!

The Moon is much closer to Earth than stars and other planets are. But the Moon is still far away. About thirty Earths could fit between Earth and the Moon.

Moving Away

The Moon's orbit is getting farther from Earth. It is moving about 1.5 inches (3.8 cm) away each year. That is about how fast your nails grow!

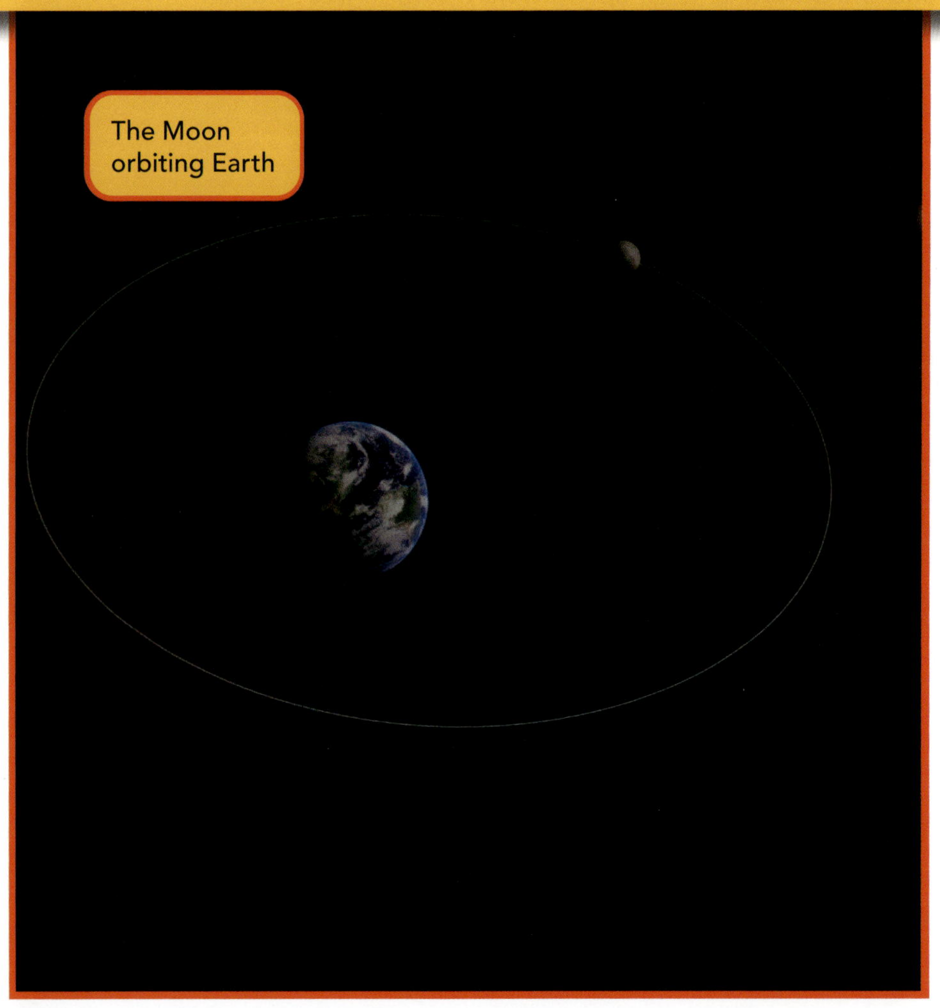

The Moon orbiting Earth

Astronaut Gene Cernan wears a spacesuit during a 1972 spacewalk.

An atmosphere surrounds Earth. It includes the oxygen we need to breathe. But the Moon has almost no atmosphere. Humans can't breathe there without a spacesuit or a spacecraft.

There is less gravity on the Moon than on Earth. Objects fall to the ground more slowly on the Moon. People even weigh less on the Moon than they do on Earth!

Phases of the Moon

Think of the Moon as a big cookie. Sometimes the Moon looks like a full cookie. Other times it looks like half of a cookie or a cookie with a big bite taken out of it. But the Moon is always a full cookie even when it doesn't look like it.

As the Moon goes around Earth, different parts of the Moon are lit up. We see the Moon as different shapes. These shapes are called phases of the Moon. The bright areas of the Moon are in daytime. The dark areas are in nighttime.

The diagram on the right page shows the Moon phases. The center ring shows the Moon as it moves around Earth. The outer ring shows how the Moon looks from Earth during each phase.

The Moon phases

First Quarter
Waxing Gibbous
Waxing Crescent
Full
New
Waning Gibbous
Waning Crescent
Third Quarter

CHAPTER 2

THE MOON'S SURFACE

You can see the Moon from Earth at night and sometimes during the day. The Moon does not make its own light. The light you see is sunlight that is bouncing off the Moon.

Dark and Light Areas

The Moon has dark areas and light areas. Light areas are highlands. They are older parts of the moon. Dark areas are maria. They are younger parts of the moon.

The Moon as seen from Earth

Highlands are higher areas than maria. They have more impact craters. Impact craters are made when space rocks hit the ground at high speeds. Dirt and rocks fly out and leave behind a hole shaped like a bowl.

Maria are smoother and lower areas than highlands. Maria formed from large space rocks hitting the Moon. The space rocks left giant round holes that filled with lava from volcanoes.

This image shows a mare (*bottom left*) and highlands (*upper right*).

From Earth, we always see the same side of the Moon. We call that side the near side. The side we don't see from Earth is the far side. The far side has fewer maria than the near side.

The near side (*left*) and far side (*right*) of the Moon

The Moon's Far Side

In 1959, humans saw the far side of the Moon for the first time. A spacecraft flew around the Moon and took pictures of the far side.

The Moon's cratered surface as seen by the Apollo 10 spacecraft

Tycho crater

Impact Craters

The Moon is covered in impact craters. Smaller ones are bowl-shaped. Larger ones can be flat on the bottom or have mountains. Some even have rings of mountains.

On Earth, craters disappear over time. Water and wind slowly destroy or bury them. But the Moon has no atmosphere and no liquid water, so craters can last for billions of years.

Hot and Cold

The Moon can be very hot and very cold. The Moon's equator can reach 250°F (121°C) in the daytime. It can drop to -208°F (-133°C) during the nighttime.

The Moon's north and south poles are even colder. The poles can drop to -410°F (-246°C). The insides of some craters there are always covered in shadows. There is even water ice in some of the craters.

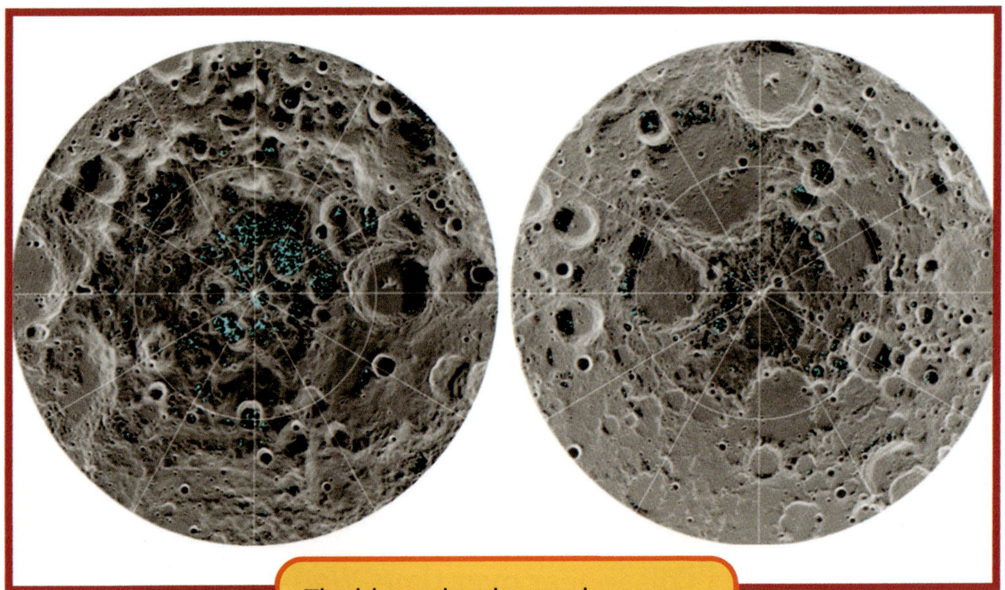

The blue color shows where water ice is near the Moon's south pole (*left*) and north pole (*right*).

Astronauts of the Apollo 15 mission visited mountains and the Hadley Rille lava channel.

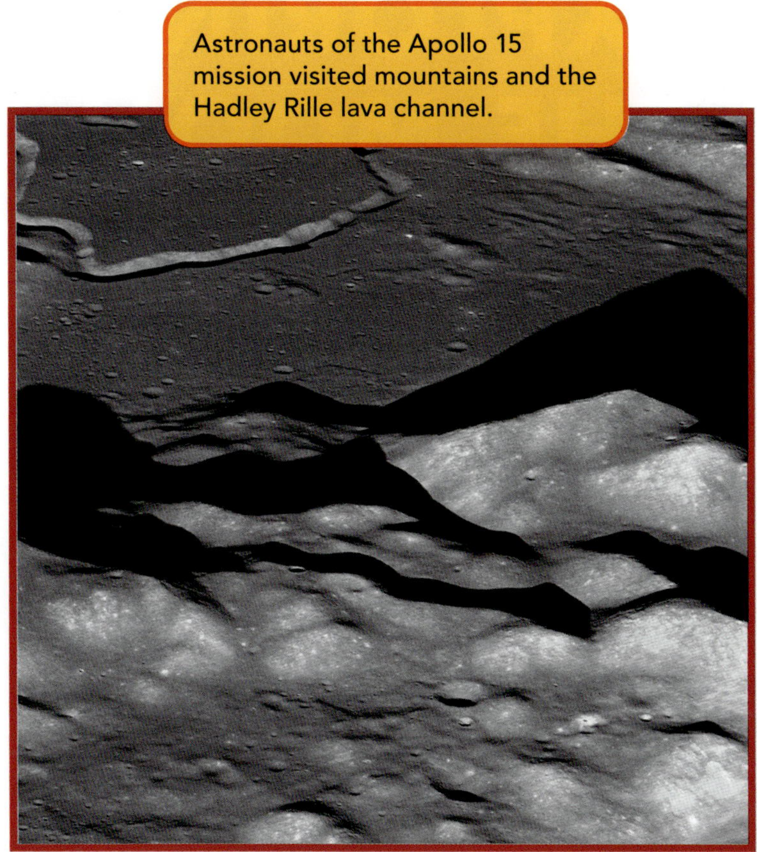

Mountains and Valleys

The Moon has valleys and mountains. It also has rilles. They look like dry rivers. They were formed long ago by hot, flowing lava.

CHAPTER 3

EXPLORING THE MOON

More than one hundred spacecraft have been made to explore the Moon. Some never reached the Moon, but many of them did. They have taken pictures and gathered info to learn about the Moon.

Artwork of the Lunar Reconnaissance Orbiter, which has been orbiting the Moon since 2009

Orbiters, landers, and rovers are kinds of spacecraft. Orbiters circle the Moon. Landers land on the Moon's surface, and rovers drive on the surface to study it up close.

People began using robotic spacecraft to explore the Moon in the 1960s. The first spacecraft flew by the Moon. They helped us learn how to land humans on the Moon. In 1969, astronauts even visited the lander that had arrived at their landing site more than two years before.

Astronaut Pete Conrad of the Apollo 12 mission visits robotic lander Surveyor 3.

Apollo Missions

The Moon is the only place other than Earth that people have visited. Twelve astronauts walked on the Moon during six of the National Aeronautics and Space Administration (NASA) Apollo missions between 1969 and 1972.

Astronauts got to the Moon using the Saturn V, a powerful rocket. After launch, astronauts took about three days to get to the Moon.

A Saturn V launching the Apollo 11 mission on July 16, 1969

The image *Earthrise* taken on December 24, 1968

The first human moon mission was Apollo 8. It was a test of the Saturn V and the spacecraft it carried. Astronauts Jim Lovell, Frank Borman, and William Anders orbited the Moon.

Anders took the picture *Earthrise* while the spacecraft traveled around the Moon. *Earthrise* is a famous picture where Earth appears to rise from behind the Moon.

In 1969, Neil Armstrong and Buzz Aldrin became the first humans to walk on the Moon. They were part of the Apollo 11 mission. Michael Collins was the third astronaut on the mission. Collins stayed in orbit around the Moon while Armstrong and Aldrin explored the surface.

Buzz Aldrin preparing to step onto the Moon

Aldrin placing a tool near the Apollo 11 lander

Aldrin on the Moon

Astronaut Harrison Schmitt of the Apollo 17 mission collects Moon rocks and dirt.

Astronauts set up tools on the Moon during the Apollo missions. Scientists used the tools to study the Moon.

The astronauts also collected Moon rocks and dirt to bring back for scientists to study on Earth. The Apollo missions returned about 842 pounds (382 kg) of Moon rocks and dirt to Earth. That is about the weight of five adults.

Black Sky

The sky is always black on the Moon. That is because the Moon has no atmosphere. On Earth, sunlight bounces around in the atmosphere to create our blue sky.

After Apollo 11, there were five more Apollo Moon landings. The last three missions each had a small car called the Lunar Roving Vehicle. Astronauts drove the Lunar Rover to explore more of the Moon's surface.

The Apollo 17 Lunar Roving Vehicle

Schmitt near a large boulder and the Apollo 17 Lunar Roving Vehicle

The Moon rocks and dirt brought back by the Apollo missions taught us many things. They also gave evidence to support the idea that the Moon formed from a giant impact over four billion years ago.

This idea says that a small planet hit Earth. Parts of Earth and the planet flew into space. Most of the parts fell back to Earth. But some of it stuck together and formed the Moon.

This artwork shows the giant impact that led to the Moon forming.

Earth as seen from the Moon by the Lunar Reconnaissance Orbiter in 2015

Future Moon Missions

Since the Apollo missions, many countries have explored the Moon with orbiters, landers, and rovers. Some spacecraft are exploring the Moon now. More countries plan to send spacecraft to the Moon in the future.

NASA is also working on future human missions. NASA's Artemis program plans to send the first woman and first person of color to the Moon. It also plans to build a base camp on the Moon.

Having humans walk on the Moon for the first time since 1972 will be exciting. Would you want to go to the Moon?

The Moon in enhanced color

NASA's Space Launch System rocket launches in 2022 for a test flight. The rocket is planned to take humans back to the Moon.

Glossary

atmosphere: the gases surrounding a planet, moon, or other body

equator: the imaginary circle around a planet or moon that is halfway between the north and south poles

highland: a brighter, higher, older, more cratered area on the Moon

impact crater: a bowl-shaped hole caused by space rocks hitting the ground at high speeds

lava: hot liquid rock that flows out of a volcano, then cools and hardens into solid rock

mare (plural: maria): a darker, younger, less cratered area on the Moon

orbit: the path a planet, moon, or other object follows as it goes around another object

spacecraft: a vehicle or object made for travel in outer space. Robotic spacecraft do not have people onboard.

Learn More

Betts, Bruce, PhD. *Casting Shadows: Solar and Lunar Eclipses with The Planetary Society®*. Minneapolis: Lerner Publications, 2024.

Britannica Kids: Moon
https://kids.britannica.com/kids/article/Moon/353489

Hirsch, Rebecca E. *Mysteries of the Moon*. Minneapolis: Lerner Publications, 2021.

Huddleston, Emma. *Explore the Moon*. Minneapolis: Kids Core, 2022.

NASA Space Place: All about the Moon
https://spaceplace.nasa.gov/all-about-the-moon/en/

The Planetary Society: The Moon
https://www.planetary.org/worlds/the-moon

Index

Photo Acknowledgments

Images credits: F. Scott Schafer/The Planetary Society, p. 2; grayjay/Shutterstock, p. 4; NASA/JPL-Caltech, pp. 6-7, 26; Garor/Shutterstock, p. 8; NASA, pp. 9, 15 (top)-16, 18, 20-22 (bottom); Elena11/Shutterstock, p. 10; NASA/Bill Dunford, p. 11; Bruce Betts, p. 12; NASA/GSFC/Arizona State University, pp. 13, 27; NASA/Goddard Space Flight Center/Arizona State University, p. 14 (left and right); NASA/Wikimedia Commons (PD), pp. 15 (bottom), 19, 22 (top)-25 (top and bottom); NASA/Goddard/Arizona State University, p. 17; NASA/JPL/USGS, p. 28; NASA/Bill Ingalls, p. 29. Cover: NASA/Goddard Space Flight Center/Arizona State University.

For my sons, Daniel and Kevin, and for all the members of The Planetary Society®

Lerner Publications Company
An imprint of Lerner Publishing Group, Inc.
241 First Avenue North
Minneapolis, MN 55401 USA

For reading levels and more information, look up this title at www.lernerbooks.com.

Main body text set in Aptifer Sans LT Pro. Typeface provided by Linotype AG.

Editor: Brianna Kaiser **Designer:** Mary Ross

Library of Congress Cataloging-in-Publication Data

Names: Betts, Bruce (PhD), author.
Title: The Moon : our nearest neighbor / Bruce Betts, PhD.
Description: Minneapolis, MN : Lerner Publications , [2025] | Series: Exploring our solar system with the Planetary Society | Includes bibliographical references and index. | Audience: Ages 7–10 | Audience: Grades 2–3 | Summary: "Scientists are always learning more about Earth's Moon. And more trips to the Moon are being planned! From the Moon's size to its surface features, readers will love learning all about our close space neighbor"— Provided by publisher.
Identifiers: LCCN 2024009483 (print) | LCCN 2024009484 (ebook) | ISBN 9798765648308 (library binding) | ISBN 9798765661758 (paperback) | ISBN 9798765654675 (epub)
Subjects: LCSH: Moon—Juvenile literature.
Classification: LCC QB582 .B48 2025 (print) | LCC QB582 (ebook) | DDC 523.3—dc23/eng/20240326

LC record available at https://lccn.loc.gov/2024009483
LC ebook record available at https://lccn.loc.gov/2024009484

Manufactured in the United States of America
1-1011035-53388-5/30/2024